The Story of Ruth
THE ROMANCE OF REDEMPTION

D1500628

By
Bobby Conner

Table of Contents

Introduction

Concealed deep in the Old Testament Scripture, tucked away among the massive history books of the Old Covenant, is the tiny Book of Ruth, one of the most engaging and endearing love stories in recorded history. Romance, drama, intrigue, swift moving action and interesting personalities are all found in the Book of Ruth. In this book you will see God's goodness displayed in the most difficult of times. And, after careful study we must conclude that the Book of Ruth is more than an interesting and inspired book of history. It is His story—the story of Christ Jesus and His lasting love for His Church.

Ruth lived during the dark days of the Judges when Israel was far away from God and sin was rampant. However, God's providential care is very evident as He brings Ruth out of Moab in order to bring her in to His purposes. The Spirit of God will release much needed hope and assurance into the heart of all who will take time to study this fascinating story of Ruth's redemption.

This book still captivates hearts and inspires hope. This ancient romance in the harvest fields of Israel has a deep prophetic meaning for the Church today. In its pages we discover a powerful prophetic message for the end-time Church.

I want to suggest three reasons why the Book of Ruth was written. The first is to give the genealogy of Jesus Christ. Ruth was the great-grandmother of David. Many believe that the Book of Ruth was written to provide a record of this historical background.

A second reason is the picture of redemption which is so beautifully painted in the Book of Ruth. Boaz appears as the kinsman-redeemer who redeemed his Gentile bride; Ruth is a type of the Church, the Bride of Christ.

Third, the Book of Ruth was written to stir in our hearts a pure passion for a living relationship with Christ Jesus. This is because Jesus has bought us and He has brought us out of the land of death and darkness, placing us in His Kingdom of love and light.

A Prophetic Perspective of the Book of Ruth

Many of us have undoubtedly read and enjoyed the Book of Ruth. It truly is a wonderful and historical love story, however, the Book of Ruth is much more than that. As we focus our attention on the allegorical meaning, we will marvel at the wonderful prophetic truths that are hidden in this romance. I want to encourage you to press into the Lord and ask Him to give you revelation and inspiration as you read. Ask the Spirit of Truth to speak to you.

We will discover profound biblical insights as the Holy Spirit unlocks the hidden truths. This book is much more than a courtship between two lovers. It signifies the coming of Jesus Christ and the restoration of the Church. It's a divine love story with astonishing prophetic insight for your life. In "type," we are beholding the beautiful relationship of the Church, the Bride of Christ, to the Lord Jesus Christ, our heavenly Boaz.

The Book of Ruth is an incredible revelation that is refreshing as well as rewarding. The Book of Ruth is a prophetic message from the heart of God to His Church. You will rejoice, clearly seeing God's sovereign grace bringing redemption and restoration as well as intimate relationship. Your heart will experience God's overwhelming love and power as He brings Ruth into a lasting relationship with Himself.

Seeing God's goodness and grace extended to Ruth will result in our joining testimonies with the Prophet Nahum as he declares, "God is good, a stronghold in the day of trouble and He knows all who are trusting Him" (see Nahum 1:7). We will also join the Psalmist when he pronounced, "God is a very present help in the time of trouble." The promise is revealed in Scripture that God desires to bless His people and bring them to a good end (see Jeremiah 29:11). The Word of God reveals the desire of God: "Beloved, I wish above all things that you may prosper and be in health..." (see III John 2:2). God longs to see His people blessed.

The Book of Ruth is a fascinating journey. Faith will increase as you realize God will make a way for you where there seems to be no way. Like Ruth, your start might have been rocky and hard, nonetheless, God can turn things around. This is never more evident than in the life of Ruth, the Moabitess, born in a pagan land yet redeemed and placed in the lineage of Christ the King. Through this story we will discover that God has a wonderful plan for His people and He will provide all that is needed to accomplish this plan.

Ruth's beginning was not very pleasant. She was a young widow living in a pagan land without any means of support, yet by God's grace and favor things radically changed for her. The promises of God's word are steadfast and sure, stating that when a person puts their trust in God they are, **"...a new creation; old things passed away; behold, all things become new" (II Corinthians 5:17).** Because God is for us, who can truly stand against us? We know that in Christ we *are* more than victorious.

In this book you will quickly discover help and hope which will release great encouragement. This book will release the understanding that no matter how desperate a situation we find ourselves in, God has a wonderful destiny for each of us and He can and will bring us out of despair into delight and from gloom to amazing grace, if we will turn to Him.

Open wide your heart and soul as you find yourself caught up into one of the most interesting and heartening books in all of Scripture. This is an extremely important message for each of us. Take your time as you read this story and allow your heart to meditate upon the redemptive grace of God, seeing how precious His plans are for mankind.

This saga reveals God's wondrous plan to redeem our life from the land of death and destruction (Moab), bringing us out of the "land of lack"where we have been living on leftovers which are stale anointings, and into the "land of grace and favor." Pastors and leadership take heart: God is bringing the Church out of Moab and we are beginning to experience deliverance from the land of lack and leftovers. For too long the Church has been living on leftovers, just getting by on past anointings and what others have discarded. We should appreciate those who have gone before us and all they have accomplished. However, it is time to move out from of the edge of the field and into the center of fruitfulness. This is where the fresh handfuls of our purpose will be discovered. He is bringing us into the Lord's land of grace and favor, where He commands His reapers to place handfuls of purpose and provision in our grasp.

This story seems to be a paradox in one sense. The more Ruth's freedom of experience narrows, the more God's favor is revealed in her life. It is very important that we understand the process of God's pruning. He permits pruning to occur in our lives in order that we might bear more and better fruit. And so, this is how the story of Ruth unfolds. Ruth is brought from a country to a city, from a city to a field, and from a field to a threshing floor. Then Ruth is brought from a threshing floor to a city gate and from a city gate into a marriage bed. It was through this constantly confining journey, this form of pruning, that God brought this woman from a land of wicked idolatry into a place of relationship and redemption. The fruit of these events is that she became the great-grandmother of King David, thus receiving a place in the lineage of Christ Jesus.

Each time Ruth's movement is restricted she experiences an increase in the grace and favor of the Lord. The

Lord deals with each of us in this same manner. As we release more and more of our will to Him, the more of God's freedom (His grace and favor) we experience. Remember, "Where the Spirit of the Lord is, there is freedom" (see II Corinthians 3:17). God's truth releases freedom (see John 8:32). The Book of Ruth is a story of restoration and redemption resulting from relationship.

You will be encouraged knowing no matter what your beginning was, God can turn your situation around. This is very evident from the story of Ruth.

He Brought Us Out—To Bring Us In

A continuous theme throughout the Book of Ruth is, "He brought us out—to bring us in." That passage comes from Deuteronomy 6:23 and it says, **"He brought us out from there, that He might bring us in, to give us the land of which He swore to our fathers."** These words are demonstrated in the eighth book of the Bible, the Book of Ruth. The number eight speaks of new beginnings. The Book of Ruth is the "now" prophetic word to the Body of Christ that is readying us for the turn of events that eight speaks of. Truly the Body of Christ stands poised at the threshold of a brand new day. Isaiah 48:6-7 reveals that God is about to do a brand new thing.

"He brought us out…" I'm so glad we are out—out of the world of sin, out of bondage and the life the devil had for us. Now, He wants to bring us into the life that God has for us.

To help understand the entire story we will begin at the end of the book. Look at Ruth 4:13. Many say you should build up to the climax of a story, but beginning at the end of the story will help give us understanding.

So Boaz took Ruth, and she was his wife: and when he went in to her, the LORD gave her conception, and she bare a son (Ruth 4:13).

This is what God is really looking for. God is looking for an intimate relationship between Ruth (the Church) and Boaz (the Lord Jesus Christ) and He wants an impregnation and a birth.

So, what is the result of this union between Boaz and Ruth?

And the women, her neighbors gave it a name saying, 'There is a son born to Naomi' and they called his name Obed ... (Ruth 4:17).

Obed (who was, of course, the child born to Ruth) means, "the one with the servant's heart."

As you read Chapter One, it is important to remember that "He brought us out to bring us in" and the number one thing God wants is relationship that brings forth good fruit.

The Lord is about to bring forth a servant out of the Church. He is about to change the entire paradigm of the Church and we will have a servant's heart instead of having the heart of one that always demands to be served. We will have the mentality to serve and that is the way we get to the top—we serve our way to the top! In this study we will initially look at the problems, the places, and the people.

11

Chapter One

The biblical names of places and characters in the Book of Ruth are filled with prophetic revelation. We will miss much of the significance of the story from God's viewpoint if we do not understand the names. Reading Ruth from an earthly viewpoint gives us factual and historical information—reading it from God's perspective helps us understand the heavenly truths that God wants to communicate to us.

The opening setting for the Book of Ruth is the town of Bethlehem-Judah. The name characterizes life as a place of bountiful provision and joy. Unfortunately, we observe from the narrative that the people in Bethlehem-Judah are presently suffering from famine.

The Problems, The Places, and The People

Now it came to pass in the days when the judges ruled, that there was a famine in the land. And a certain man of Bethlehem-Judah went to sojourn in the country of Moab, he, and his wife, and his two sons.

> **And the name of the man was Elimelech, and the name of his wife Naomi, and the name of his two sons Mahlon and Chilion, Ephrathites of Bethlehem-Judah. And they came into the country of Moab, and continued there (Ruth 1:1-2).**

Elimelech is a Hebrew man whose name has an awesome meaning, which is, "Almighty God is my King." It doesn't take long to discover that he falls short of living up to what his name implies. He has a wonderful and faithful wife named Naomi, whose name means "the pleasant one" and two sons. Naomi's name also carries allegorical significance as it relates to the Scriptures, which teach that the knowledge of God is pleasant. The writer of Proverbs declared, **"When wisdom entereth into thine heart, and knowledge is pleasant unto thy soul; Discretion shall preserve thee, understanding shall keep thee" (Proverbs 2:10-11).** Again he declared that, **"Her ways are ways of pleasantness, and all her paths are peace" (Proverbs 3:17).**

We observe Elimelech as he is sadly looking across the landscape with his head throbbing, his heart troubled and bewildered, and his lips parched, cracked, and swollen. His eyes are reddened and matted with dirt. They are virtually forced shut by the constant hot, dusty wind whipping the dry sand across the barren, sun-baked land. The parched ground can yield nothing. Its only harvest is the blinding and choking dust. No rain is in sight and no food; famine has plagued the land of Bethlehem-Judah. He asks, "What will I do to escape this time of drought?"

In bewilderment Elimelech is about to make a choice that will change his family's life forever. In his desperate dilemma he makes the ill-fated decision to take his family and flee from the famine into the land of Moab. This mistake will one day bring premature death to himself and to his sons, Mahlon and Chilion. Beware of making decisions based on sight and not on faith, for they lead to danger and deception. As leaders in our families we too must be very careful not to make decisions that will cause our families to walk in darkness. We must pray and be lead by the Spirit of God—not cater to the directions of our mind.

We learn several more things from reading these verses. We know they lived in Bethlehem-Judah. Bethlehem means "house of bread" and Judah means, "place of praise." So, they are moving from a place of provision and praise into a place called Moab. Moab is not a good place to go—no one in their right mind would want to raise their children in a place like Moab.

Verse 1 says they **"went to sojourn"** and verse 2 says they **"continued there."** Do you believe that people often say they aren't going to make whatever they are doing a lifestyle, that it's just something they are going to get into for the short term? You can see that happening here. It says they went to take a trip, they went to sojourn, and then they ended up staying or continuing there. Later we find out they lived there at least ten years.

Most of us have asked this question at one time or another, especially when we are distraught: "How did I ever end up here?" That is a very appropriate question to ask about Elimelech and Naomi: "How did they end-up in Moab?"

I know many people drop out of churches with this same short-term attitude, never intending to make it a permanent change. They say, "I'm an adult, I can get involved in anything, it's not going to overtake me." So, like Elimelech, they go to sojourn in Moab and end up continuing there.

A Time to Plea—Not a Time to Flee!

It is always a downward spiral when we leave the "house of bread" and the "place of praise." That is never the plan of God. When trouble comes, it is not a time to run away from God, it is a time to run to Him. The time of famine was an open invitation to pray to the Living God. God said that if He shut up the heavens and there was no rain, that His people were to pray and He would hear and send rain (see II Chronicles 7:14). Believers are not excused from adversity and hardships. However, our adversity leads us to make a choice to live by faith and pray, or to run away from God and live with the consequence. When a famine or a hardship comes, it's not a time to flee— it is a time to plea. It's not a time to run. It's a time to pray.

Believers, we are not exempt from trials and hardship. It is imperative that we discover the importance of running to the Lord, and not from His help, when adversity arises. Hardships can make us bitter or better; we hold the key by our action and reactions. If we learn to yield and surrender to the Lord during adversity, those times can be an opportunity for great spiritual advancement. It is a wise move to let hardships drive you closer to the Lord. Do not allow it to cause you to retreat from the Lord. God alone is a very present help in the time of trouble. We must keep our focus upon Him (see Psalms 121:1-2). We must learn that God is our refuge and strength (see Psalms 46:1). As we keep our focus upon God we will have lasting peace (see Isaiah 26:3).

The Scripture states that God brought us out in order to bring us into the land that He had promised (see Deuteronomy 6:22-23). It is not a time to be sidetracked but a time to stay on course. We must go on to know the Lord.

We should never allow desperation to move us to defy the Word of God. This man, Elimelech, does just that; he moves his family into a pagan place. It is a tragedy for this Hebrew family to move from Bethlehem-Judah to Moab. It was a downward journey that lead them to dryness and barrenness.

Bethlehem of Judea means, "house of bread." Doesn't that sound good? Isn't it marvelous that the Lord Jesus Christ is in the house and He is serving? He's serving the bread of His presence. I've been in meetings when the whole room begins to smell like fresh baked bread because the Lord has stepped in, and He's serving the bread of His presence. One of the breads that He is serving is healing. Remember that "healing is the children's bread."

Once again, Elimelech's name means, "Almighty God is my King." He represents those who talk the talk, but they don't walk the walk. There are many people that will emphatically tell you that they are a Christian, if you ask them. So, Elimelech's name means that God is his King or Provider, but when the famine comes, instead of turning to God and letting God be who He says He is, he turns and carries his family into a pagan place called Moab.

Moab's Origin

The nation of Moab was situated along the eastern border of the Dead Sea, on the plateau between the Dead Sea and the Arabian Desert. It is not a very big place—about 35 miles long and 25 miles wide. It was primarily a high plateau; Moab also had mountainous areas and deep gorges. It was a fertile area for crops and herds. During most of Israel's history, the Moabites were Israel's enemies. They caused Israel to stumble through pagan idolatry on several occasions.

The old saying, "as the twig is bent so grows the tree," is so very true in the story of Moab. His father was Lot, a man who tried to walk by sight and not by faith. Lot made his choices by what he thought would be the best for himself. He was motivated by the greed of his heart, so he led his family into a land under the curse of God—Sodom and Gomorrah. The warning is very clear, "Be not deceived; God is not mocked: whatsoever man sows, that shall he also reap." If we sow to the wind we shall reap the whirlwind. We always reap more than we sow for the harvest is always bigger than the seed that was planted. If we sow to the flesh, of the flesh we will reap corruption and death. The fruit of the "flesh" is a sour harvest—such is a crop of greed, lust and pride (see Galatians 5:19-21—the fruit of the flesh).

We discover this story revealing the heart of Lot in the Book of Genesis. "So they left Egypt, Abram with his

18

wife and Lot, and all that they owned, for Abram was very rich in livestock, silver, and gold" (see Genesis 13:1-13).

Lot sought to take what was the best for himself at all costs. Our decisions should never be made on the basis of greed or lust for the riches of this world. Lot was also very wealthy, he owned sheep and cattle, and many servants. But the land could not support both Abram and Lot with all their flocks and herds. There were too many animals for the available pasture. Fights broke out between the herdsmen of Abram and Lot, despite the danger they all faced from the tribes of Canaanites and Perizzites present in the land.

Then Abram talked it over with Lot. "This fighting between our men has got to stop," he said. "We can't afford to let a rift develop between our clans. Close relatives such as ourselves must present a united front! Take your choice of the land you want and we will separate. If you want that part over there to the east, then I'll stay here in the western section. Or if you want the west, then I'll go over there to the east" (see Genesis 13:6-9).

Lot took a long, lustful look at the fertile plains of the Jordan River which were well watered (this was before Jehovah destroyed Sodom and Gomorrah). The entire section around Zoar was beautiful. When considering what appears to be beautiful, one must be very careful to remember that Satan can transform himself into an angel of light. Not all that glitters is pure gold.

So that is what Lot chose—the Jordan valley to the east of them. He went there with his flocks and servants, and thus he and Abram parted company. Lot's heart was filled with pride knowing that he had gotten the best deal. It is sad when people can take pleasure in esteeming themselves above others and especially relatives. Abram stayed in the land of Canaan, while Lot lived among the cities of the plain, settling at a place near the city of Sodom.

The men of this area, which was called Sodom and Gomorrah, were unusually wicked and sinned greatly against God. The sin of this city had come up before God and He was ready to bring judgment upon the perversion of men having sex with men, and likewise women with women. This evil perversion had aroused the anger of Holy God.

Have you ever noticed that what we compromise with at first, doesn't take us long to condone? If you won't stand for some things, you'll fall for anything. Sin has a way of causing one's heart to grow hard and cold, soon becoming desensitized to the wickedness of a place. When Lot first got to the land of Sodom he was troubled and vexed by the wicked, perverted lifestyle of the people. However, as you read on, there came a day when he was sitting as an elder in the city gate of this perverted place. God is not at all concerned about being socially or politically correct, as Lot most certainly must have been. He is concerned with our being holy and keeping His standards. Lot's lifestyle proved very costly in the long run.

God sent a message to Abram instructing him to tell his nephew (Lot) to get out of that city because their wicked immorality has come up before His face. He is going to send down fire from Heaven to burn that city off of the face of the earth. God is not tolerant of that kind of sin. So God sends the message and He sends the angels down to Sodom and Gomorrah and the cities are destroyed.

Lot gets his wife and his two daughters out of the city and they start up the hill of Zoar. God tells them not to look back. The shortest message recorded out of the lips of Jesus Christ is "Remember Lot's wife." It's found in the Book of Luke. You and I would do very well to remember Lot's wife. God told Lot to get up, get out, and not to look back. But as they started up the hill of Zoar she looked back. Why did she look back? Because her heart never left the life she had accepted in Sodom. The pull of the old life was still there.

I know a lot of people who get into Church life, but it doesn't take them long to start to look back. The Bible says, "They went out from us because they were never a part of us"(see I John 2:19). **If any man be in Christ, he is a new creature: old things are passed away, behold, all things are become new"(II Corinthians 5:17).**

So then, Lot's wife looks back and turns into a pillar of salt, but, Lot and his two daughters make it up to Zoar. The Bible tells us in Genesis that they are in a cave in Zoar. Lot's two daughters begin to talk and here is a paraphrase of their conversation. They are talking between themselves and say, "Listen. All the big hunks are barbequed. All the big studs are toast." And they say, "Who is going to do with us the way of a man with a woman?"

Moab's Conception

The land of Moab is the result of an incestuous night between a drunken father and his daughter. The son born as a result of this evil connection is Moab, the father of the Moabite nation. We discover this recorded in Genesis 19:30-38.

Scripture tells us that after Sodom was destroyed, Lot left Zoar, fearful of the people there, and went to live in a cave in the mountains with his two daughters. One day the older girl said to her sister, "There isn't a man anywhere in this entire area, and our father will soon be too old for having children. Come, let's fill him with wine and then we will sleep with him, so that our clan will not come to an end" (see Genesis 19:31-32).

This is a sad and sick situation; here is a father made drunk and seduced by his wayward and wanting daughters. They got him drunk that night and the older girl went in and had sexual intercourse with her father, but he was too drunk to be aware of her lying down or getting up again. This secret sin of incest is a terrible problem even in our day. However, we have a loving heavenly Father that can and will extend His mercy and grace to heal the deep wounds and scars of even such deep betrayal and misuse.

The next morning she said to her younger sister, "I slept with father last night. Let's fill him with wine again tonight and you go in and lay with him so that our family line will continue" (see Genesis 19:34). So they got him drunk again the second night and the younger girl went in and lay with him and, as before, he did not know what had happened.

And so it was that both girls became pregnant by their father. This is the seedbed in which these nations were birthed—a father who was deceived, made drunk by his own daughters and then unknowingly has sex with them.

Moab's Birth

The older daughter's baby was named Moab, which means, "of his father." He became the ancestor of the nation of the Moabites. The name of the younger girl's baby was Benammi; he became the ancestor of the nation of the Ammonites.

Where did these two girls get this type of thinking? I would suggest it was the evil atmosphere that they were surrounded with in the evil land, Sodom, where their father chose to live. The Scripture declares, **"The fathers have eaten a sour grape, and the children's teeth are set on edge."(Jeremiah 31:29)** This means what we do has lasting effects upon our children and their children.

Thus, the lasting effect of living in the wrong place, in the evil land of Sodom, was an ungodly son born to Lot whom they named Moab. The land of Moab was not a place where you would want to live.

God gives this warning in Numbers 21:29, **"Woe to thee, Moab! Thou art undone, O people of Chemosh: he hath given his sons that escaped, and his daughters, into captivity unto Sihon king of the Amorites."**

Chemosh speaks of evil demon worship, which was a big problem for the Moabite people.

Again we pose the question, "Why is this man, Elimelech, now fleeing away from Bethlehem." What caused this family to flee into Moab—a place they had been forbidden to go into? The Scripture gives a clear warning: **"There is a way that seems right to a person, but the end thereof are the ways of death" (Proverbs 14:12).** There is death and destruction when one sets his heart against the will and Word of God. God's warnings are for our protection.

We should never attempt to meet needs by going against the revealed will and Word of God. We can never justify doing the right thing in the wrong way. It is plain and simple: there is just no right way to do the wrong thing. Scripture warns us that disobedience and rebellion are as the sin of witchcraft: **"For rebellion is as the sin of witchcraft, and stubbornness is as iniquity and idolatry..." (I Samuel 15:23).**

The Prophetic Message

We are still talking about the people and the place. It is always a horrible thing when we leave the "house of bread" and the "place of praise" and go into a "place of pollution."

Now, here is the prophetic message: The Book of Ruth, is symbolic of the story of the Church; Ruth represents the Church—Naomi represents the Holy Spirit—Boaz represents the Lord Jesus.

Let's continue to examine the names. We already found out that Elimelech's name means "Almighty God is my King" and that Naomi's name means the "pleasant, cordial one." Ruth means the "friendly, warm, welcoming one." Won't it be wonderful when the Church is known as the friendly, warm, welcoming one?

Do you know what the two boys, Mahlon's and Chilion's, names mean? Mahlon means, "sickness and weakness" and the Chilion means, "dying, destruction, consumption, and failing." Who in the world would have ever named their sons those names? Is it any wonder that these two young men died at such an early age? Names are extremely powerful; they carry potential for both good and evil. The power of life and death is in the tongue (see Proverbs 18:21). Each time these young men's names were spoken, Chilion was assigned consumption and destruction and Mahlon's name echoed the call for sickness and death. This *is* the reason the two died at such a young age. We must be especially careful how we name our children. We all have a way of living out what is spoken over us. So, their names were sickness and dying—did it work?

And Elimelech Naomi's husband died; and she was left, and her two sons.

And they took them wives of the women of Moab; the name of the one was Orpah, and the name of the other, Ruth: and they dwelled there about ten years.

And Mahlon and Chilion died also both of them; and the woman was left of her two sons and her husband (Ruth 1:3-5).

We have a desperate situation here. The dad is dead, the two boys are dead, and now Naomi is responsible for her two daughters-in-law, Orpah and Ruth. Orpah means "desert gazelle." Literally, when you take her name apart it means "the one that is quick to flee." Have you ever seen a deer out in a field? If you startle one, it will be gone in a moment. That's what this word means; one that is quick to flee. Does she live up to that? We find that she does. We find out about the power of choice here because of names given (and lived out) and decisions made.

Our choices really mean a great deal. Many people think, "Well, if God wants to save me, He'll save me." No! You'll go straight to hell thinking like that. God's doing everything He can to save you. God is not willing that any should perish, but that all should come to repentance (see II Peter 3:9). If you go to hell, you'll go to hell over everything that God has set in your way.

Here are two girls, Ruth and Orpah, apparently the same age, raised in the same neighborhood and environment and they both have the same chance to succeed or fail. Additionally, both girls had the same fellowship and union with Naomi. But one of them is going to make a wise choice and one of them will make a terribly wrong choice. The power of choice is very important. **"...choose you this day whom ye will serve"(Joshua 24:15).** "I have set before you blessings and curses; choose blessings(see Deuteronomy 11:26-32). It is true; you really have the opportunity to make the choice as to the direction you take in life. "Well," you say, "I've had a terrible life; a real bad life." Choose not to have a bad life! Choose to believe the Lord and choose to believe what He says.

There's Bread in the House

Both of the sons and the husband are dead and the three ladies are down in this pagan place. Now, look at what happens in verse 6. Remember that Naomi is a "type" of the Holy Spirit. The Holy Spirit is always listening to hear what the Father is saying and doing.

>**Then she arose with her daughters-in-law, that she might return from the county of Moab: for she had heard in the country of Moab how the Lord had visited his people in giving them bread (Ruth 1:6).**

The famine is over and she hears the report that bread is back in the house. I want to join Naomi in reporting that God is again visiting His house with fresh bread. He is back in the house. Mark 2:1 says, **"...It was noised that he was in the house."**

This is a report we must spread to others concerning the House of God. God is moving in the Church again with fresh bread. It is time to announce that the Lord's presence and power is returning to the House of God. The famine for hearing the Word of God is over for all who will seek to have their heart opened to the Spirit of Truth as He reveals the bread of Heaven. This is a time to have the eyes of your heart flooded with divine, revelatory light (see Ephesians 1:1-18). Remember, as we walk in the light as He is in the light, we will have fellowship one with another. The Word of God will release great light upon our pathway (see Psalms 119:105, 130).

So, all the way down in this pagan place Naomi hears that He's back in the house in Bethlehem. The distance from Bethlehem to Moab was about 100 miles and most of the journey was over a mountain that was a mile or more high. That is a long way. They didn't have an SUV, or a bus, and there was no train; so how did they get there?

They walked. All three of the women begin the journey back to where there is bread.

> **Wherefore she went forth out of the place where she was, and her two daughters-in-law with her; and they went on the way to return unto the land of Judah (Ruth 1:7)**.

It is wonderful to get on the way. I know a lot of people that get on their way, but they never finish. They get on their way, they join a church, they shake a preacher's hand, they go through a baptismal pool; but they never finish. So, Naomi and the girls are on their way to return to the land of praise, the land of Judah.

Why Are You Following Me?

So, they start out on their journey and Naomi tells them that if they think they are going to follow her to get something out of her, it won't work. That's what she tells them in Ruth 1:8-11. And they tell her that they are with her all the way. Have you ever heard that one before? I have been in deacon's meetings and board meetings where people said, "Oh Pastor, we are with you all the way." Watch out for those types of people.

Next, Naomi is going to do something and this is exactly where we are right now. This is where the true test comes into play.

> **And Naomi said, Turn again, my daughters: why will ye go with me? are there yet any more sons in my womb, that they may be your husbands? (Ruth 1:11)**.

Naomi basically says to these two girls, "Hey girls, if you are just following me because you think you are going to get something out of me, you better think again because you are going to be disappointed" (see Ruth 1:11).

Turn again, my daughters, go your way; for I am too old to have an husband. If I should say, I have hope; if I should have an husband also to night, and should also bear sons;

Would ye tarry for them till they were grown? would ye stay for them from having husbands? nay, my daughters; for it grieveth me much for your sakes that the hand of the LORD is gone out against me (Ruth 1:12-13).

Many people come to a church thinking they are going to get something out of it. Naomi says to these two girls, "Do you think that you are going to follow me and that I am going to find a man, fall in love with him, get pregnant, bare a son, raise him up, give him to you as a husband and do the same thing again for both of you girls? If that's what you think, you are following me foolishly" (see Ruth 1:11-13).

You would be surprised how many people are going to drop out of the Church because they thought they were going to get something out of it. That's where we are right now—there is a shifting and a shaking, a turning and a whirling going on. We will find out that we were created to serve Him and not for Him to serve us. We are the clay and He is the potter. We have preached such a low level of the Gospel until the clay is now saying to the Potter, "Hey! What are you doing?" I'll tell you, we are going to have to be still while we are on the wheel. If we get brittle, we're broken.

So she says to them, **"Turn again, my daughters..."** She tells them, again, that she won't be able to give them what they are looking for in Ruth1:12-13.

Orpah's Wrong Choice

> **And they lifted up their voice, and wept again: and Orpah kissed her mother-in-law, but Ruth clave unto her (Ruth 1:14).**

The next words are Naomi's speaking to Ruth.

> **...Behold, thy sister-in-law is gone back unto her people, and unto her gods: return thou after thy sister in law (Ruth 1:15).**

There goes Orpah, old "quick to flee." You will never hear another word in the Bible about her. This is the last word you will ever hear about Orpah. Do you know where she is at right now? She is in hell right now because she went back to her people and to her gods.

It is sad, but all too often true that many start out on the "Christian journey." However, because they are never fully committed to following the Lord, they often turn back to their old way of life when hardships arise. The Scripture says, **"They went out from us, but they were not of us; for if they had been of us, they would no doubt have continued with us..." (II Corinthians 5:17).**

It is sad to learn that Orpah returned to her people and to her gods. What a tragedy to be so near to a new life and then miss it because of a poor choice. Many people will one day regret their lost opportunity for salvation. Felix, in the Book of Acts, reported, **"Almost thou persuadest me to become a Christian"(Acts 26:28).** The rich young ruler ran and knelt at the feet of Christ but went away sad, having said no to the call of Christ, because he was too concerned about all of his possessions he would have to give up.

I beg you to make the right choice—choose Christ Jesus, the Lord. I have never spoken to anyone that said they wished they had never given their life to Christ. As a Christian minister for over thirty-two years, I have spoken to many people who did say, "I am so sorry that it took me so long to repent and give my life to Christ. I only wish I had done it sooner." "Behold, today is the day of salvation." Behold, now is the right time to make your salvation sure.

One of the gods of the Moabites was Chemosh. If you were to study about Chemosh, you would learn that he is a very diabolical, demonic pagan god. The people of Moab took the flesh of their children and burned it and gave it to him. This was a terrible pagan practice. Orpah went back to that and she is in hell today for that very reason. Both women were walking shoulder to shoulder with the same Naomi. Both had the same choice, didn't they? Ruth made the wise choice and Orpah made the wrong choice. Do you see it?

Ruth's Wise Choice

Look at Ruth 16:1. Here is that great statement Ruth made. This is the best choice she ever made. It was

31

this statement that released divine destiny into her life.

> **And Ruth said, Entreat me not to leave thee, or to return from following after thee: for whither thou goest, I will go; and where thou lodgest, I will lodge: thy people shall be my people, and thy God shall be my God (Ruth 1:16).**

We do not know all that went on down in Moab those ten plus years that they were there, but somehow, Naomi came to know and stayed true to the Living God. There was a "winning witness" there in Moab that was impregnating the heart of Ruth. Do you see it? She said, "Where you go, I will go, where you live, I will live; your people will be my people and your God will be my God." Somehow she had seen the Living Light in Naomi.

It is very important to notice in the Book of Ruth, how many times the statement is recorded, **"...and Ruth said!..."** or **"...and Ruth, the Moabitess, said..."** Ruth begins here to speak words of faith and victory, and as she speaks, what she speaks begins to come to pass. Old Covenant Scripture tells us, **"Thou shalt also decree a thing, and it shall be established unto thee: and the light shall shine upon thy ways" (Job 22:28).** The Lord Jesus agrees, **"...and shall not doubt in his heart, but shall believe that those things which he saith shall come to pass; he shall have whatsoever he saith. Therefore, I say unto you, What things soever ye desire, when ye pray, believe that ye receive them, and ye shall have them" (Mark 11:23-24).** Those good things happened for her because of God's Word and those things she spoke in faith.

Ruth continues:

Where thou diest, will I die, and there will I be buried: the LORD do so to me, and more also, if ought but death part thee and me (Ruth 1:17).

She said, "I want to die where you die and be buried there. May the Lord do terrible things to me if I allow anything but death to separate us." You would have to agree that Ruth was fully committed to this journey with Naomi.

Commitment is absolutely essential if we are to truly advance in the Kingdom of God. Sometimes it seems that the Lord will test our commitment to make sure that we truly do want to follow Him. A bold example of this is found in Song of Solomon when the Lover conceals Himself behind the lattice work to see if His beloved will take time to look for Him (see Song of Solomon 2:9). The Lord Jesus is looking for volunteer lovers. He could have made us all love and serve Him. Yet, His heart's desire is for us to desire Him.

A further example of this desire of the Lord is when the resurrected Jesus walked with the two men on the Emmaus road. As they drew near to their home, Christ made as though He would leave them and continue traveling on. However, they began to ask Him to turn aside and visit in their house. This was His plan all along; however, He wanted them to seek Him (see Luke 24:13-32).

> **When she saw that she was steadfastly minded to go with her, then she left speaking unto her (Ruth 1:18).**

Naomi stopped telling her to leave and let Ruth come with her.

An Entire City is Shaken

If this next portion of Scripture was not in the Holy Bible, you would never make me believe it. Here are two women, Naomi and Ruth, and they have been walking for many days. I don't really know how long, but these two have been walking one hundred miles up hill. They come stumbling into town and look at what happens. Remember that all three started the journey together in verse 7.

> **So they two went until they came to Bethlehem. And it came to pass, when they were come to Bethlehem, that all the city was moved about them, and they said, Is this Naomi? (Ruth 1:19).**

The entire city was moved—they were all stirred and shaken! Where had those girls been? Had they been off on some sabbatical for ten years? Were they on some "mountain top experience" with God? Had they been to seminary somewhere? No! They had been in a pagan place. But when they came back, they came back with some kind of anointing. You see, they had what you and I need.

This is the type of anointing we must have when we come into a home, school, city, or nation so that the entire place is stirred. Jesus said we were to let our light shine.

He said we were a city set on a hill that could not be hidden. Only by the power of God's Holy Spirit do we have the ability to change the spiritual atmosphere in an area.

Right now, we can't even shake a home or a church. And this says that these two shook the entire town when they walked in. The whole town said, "My God, did you feel that?" Do you believe that we should have such an awesome anointing that we would change the atmosphere? They did. I don't know about you, but I'm jealous for whatever they had. Whatever anointing they had, you and I need.

A wonderful example of someone changing the spiritual climate of a place is when Paul and Silas were in prison (see Acts 16:25-28). The Scripture records that at midnight they prayed and sang praises to God and the other prisoners heard them. Their steadfast witness under these hard conditions made a real impact on this prison because later when the earthquake came and every jail door was opened and everyone's bonds were loosed, not one single prisoner ran away. Paul was able to report to the frightened keeper, **"...we are all here."**

This same anointing must have been what was upon Peter too. For when his shadow would pass over sick people, they would be healed. I want such an anointing as that, so that when I come into a place the Lord's presence is felt. This is also what was upon the early disciples. It was reported that people saw that they were unlearned, however, they took notice of them that they had been with Jesus. This same thing is what happened to Moses when he was spending time in God's presence and his face began to shine.

Do Not Blame God

The next few verses require some explanation because they will lead you in the wrong direction if you aren't careful. This next part really needs some understanding. They are back in Bethlehem now and the entire town is saying, "Look! It's Naomi! She's back!"

...Call me not Naomi, call me Mara for the Almighty hath dealt very bitterly with me.

I went out full, and the LORD has brought me home again empty: Why then call ye me Naomi, seeing the LORD hath testified against me, and the Almighty hath afflicted me? (Ruth 1:20-21).

Here is what God told me about this passage. He said that He was tired of taking the heat for the consequences of His people's bad choices. God did not lead her into Moab—her husband Elimelech did. Elimelech was the Hebrew that claimed he knew God—he talked it, but he sure didn't walk it. Do you believe that God is going to hold people responsible for leading those that are under them into pagan places? The answer is yes. Husbands, you had better get an understanding on this thing. Do you know who lead her there? Elimelech did. He was a husband that claimed to be walking with God, but you could see as soon as the pressure was on that he went down into paganism and he did not last very long there.

So, God did not lead Naomi to Moab—her husband did. Do you understand this? I was a pastor for over 26 years and I heard the whining of the people. "Oh Pastor, my kid's on dope, my kid's this or that." Did you bring them up in the Church? Did you bring them up in the nurture and admonition of the Lord? Did you raise them righteously and demonstrate to them how to have their own relationship with the Lord? See, you can't sip the martini's at home and play your religious games on Sunday. Do you understand that as the tree is bent, so grows the tree? The Bible says that the parents eat bitter fruit and the children's teeth are set on edge, which means the children are affected by what their parents do.

So we have Naomi here telling the people not to call her Naomi, "the pleasant one," but to call her Mara "the bitter one." But God did not have any part in what happened to her. We reap what we sow. If we sow to righteousness, we reap righteousness. If we sow to the flesh, we reap of the flesh corruption. One thing about reaping is that it is always a bigger amount than that which was sown.

Barley Harvest

So Naomi returned, and Ruth the Moabitess, her daughter-in-law, with her, which returned out of the country of Moab: and they came to Bethlehem in the beginning of barley harvest (Ruth 1:22).

Here is a significant point to remember. Every harvest in the Bible deals with a dispensation of God dealing with His people—and, every harvest is mentioned in the Book of Ruth. She arrives there in Bethlehem at barley harvest. Why barley harvest? Barley was the grain that the High

Priest was to offer for the jealousy offering. It was for when a man or woman played or was even suspected of playing with adultery. We find that Ruth was there through the barley harvest, the wheat harvest, and the corn harvest. Every one of these harvests deals with a dispensation of God dealing with His people. Do you believe we are at barley harvest? Do you believe God is a jealous God? Do you believe He's tired of us playing the harlot? Do you believe that to be a "friend of the world is to be at enmity with God?" (see James 4:4-5). We need to understand that the barley harvest really means something here—every one of these harvests really means something pertinent to us.

Once I was speaking to Dr. Billy Graham about this time we are in being harvest time. He placed his weathered hand upon my shoulder and looked deep into my eyes and said, "Son, I was reared on a farm and one thing I know about harvest time—it is short. When he said that, it went off in me like a bomb. We cannot say, "There are four months and then will come the harvest." Christ said that now is the time to lift up our eyes and set our vision on the ripe harvest.

We have Naomi, the "pleasant one," and we have Ruth, the "warm and welcoming one" and they are out of Moab. Now, think of the Church. The Church is out of the "land of loose living." Do you see this is for us? God has brought us out—to bring us in. Go ahead and say that out loud. It feels good. He brought us out—to bring us in. We are out of Moab, the land of loose living. Do you think the Church has spent some time in Moab? Do you remember the early 1950's? There was scandal after scandal striking some of the big healing ministries several decades ago. Then in the early 1970's, there was scandal after scandal again due to loose living. Public scandals—loose living—Moab.

But thank God the prophetic message is that God has brought the Church out of the land of loose living. Can you guess where she is right now? The Church, right now, is where she has been during your entire lifetime. That is, living in the "land of lack and leftovers." We are living in the land of leftovers with just enough to get by. Living on what has fallen through someone else's hands. Leviticus 19:9 tells us where a stranger and a foreigner could glean—where they could get food enough to sustain them. They had to glean in the corners of the fields. They had to live on leftovers. That is where your Church has been your entire life—living on the leftover anointings. Living on what somebody else handled and misused, getting just enough to keep us alive and get us to the next place.

Chapter Two

Boaz

And Naomi had a kinsman of her husband's, a mighty man of wealth, of the family of Elimelech; and his name was Boaz (Ruth 2:1).

Boaz's name means "the sure, swift, stout, steadfast one." When I say Boaz my heart gets warm. Boaz can fix everything that needs to be fixed. He is the Lord of the harvest. He is a "type" of the Lord Jesus in this story.

When Solomon built his temple, one of the two pillars that he put in the front was named Boaz. Isn't that strange? We are going to find out that the "sure, steadfast one" is holding this whole thing up. We are going to find out that Boaz is the Lord of the harvest.

Naomi and Ruth are now back in the land of bread. The story is fantastic here.

And Ruth the Moabitess said…" (Ruth 2:2). I want you to understand that Ruth had never listened to a Kenneth Copeland tape, she had never been to a conference, but look at what she does. She begins to speak with the voice, and use the verbiage, of victory—the communication of conquering. **"And Ruth the Moabitess, said…"** her words of victory begin right here. This is really amazing. That's why it says, **"Ruth the Moabitess."** It doesn't say, "Ruth the seminary student." It clearly points out that she was from the pagan land of Moab, yet she lived by her faith.

Ruth's Faith

> **And Ruth the Moabitess said unto Naomi, Let me now go to the field, and glean ears of corn after him in whose sight I shall find grace (Ruth 2:2).**

Naomi told her to go ahead. Do you hear Ruth speaking in the language of victory here? She said, "I am going to a field and whosoever's field I end up in, there I am going to find grace." Now, we had better get a new grip and understanding on what it is we confess. You see the Bible says, **"What things soever ye desire, when ye pray, believe that ye receive them, and ye shall have them" (Mark 11:24).** See, I can get by with saying that in the Church—Mark 11:24. But, if I back up one verse, you will get mad because it says, "You will say to that mountain, be taken up and thrown into the sea—and if you will say to that mountain and not doubt whatever you say, you will have it" (see Mark 11:23). Oh no, that's just that name it and claim it stuff—but remember, Jesus said it.

Now Ruth was not whining and saying, "I'm a poor little pagan girl from a pagan place, or I'm a widow and look how young I am. How could this happen to me?" No, she said that she was going out to a field and wherever she ended up, she would find favor! She was doing what is written in Job 22. It says, "Come bring your prayers to the Lord...Decree a thing, and what you decree shall be established for you" (see Job 22:27-28). Did she decree it? Yes! So, let's watch her go.

She is out in the corner of a field. That's where she had to be according to Leviticus 19:9, which tells us that when a stranger came, he or she had to glean in the corner of the field, living in the land of leftovers. So here she is in the field doing it the right way according to the law.

And she went, and came, and gleaned in the field after the reapers: and her hap was to light on a part of the field belonging unto Boaz, who was of the kindred of Elimelech (Ruth 2:3).

Here we see the sovereign, mighty hand of God. Whose field did she end up in? Boaz's field. Now, there is only one man in the entire town who can really meet the need she has and it is Boaz. In those days they did not have a one hundred acre field with a sign on it telling them it belonged to Boaz Farms. No, there was one common field that would be broken down with a boundary marker of some kind, such as a rock. She walked out into this great big field with many different farmers there and she went directly to the right place—Boaz's field.

The King James Version says, **"her hap"** or "happened." The NIV says, **"as it turned out..."** You know it was not by chance that she ended up in his field. She was in his field because it was the field that God put her in.

The Church must start walking with purpose; with a goal and an aim. This idea of taking life as it comes is why the Church is struggling and dying. We must find the purpose for which God put us here. Otherwise we are only wasting what has been given to us by God. We must get into our destiny and stay there with determination. Many people are taking up space and they are without a cause.

So, Ruth is out there in the field. She is in the right field because it is the field that God put her in. She is out of the land of loose living. She is about to be brought out of the land of leftovers. Look at what happens next.

> **And, behold, Boaz came from Bethlehem, and said unto the reapers, The LORD be with you. And they answered him, The LORD bless thee (Ruth 2:4).**

What can you learn about Boaz here? He is a Godly man. He was not one of those Sunday morning Christians. We all know about those Sunday morning Christians, like the big boss who on Monday morning is out there cursing and belittling their workers. Not Boaz! He rides up to his workers and treats them in a wholesome way, **"The LORD be with you"** And the workers say back to him, **"The LORD bless thee."** Don't you like that? See, if you don't do your workers right, you'll never learn to do Jesus right. And you workers too—if you don't learn to do your boss right, you'll never learn to do Jesus right. These are signposts along the way.

> **Then said Boaz unto his servant that was set over the reapers, Whose damsel is this? (Ruth 2:5).**

He was saying, "Who is that in the corner?"

The Church is about to change from a "what" to a "who." The Church has been a "what" to the world. He is about to change that perception. Song of Solomon 8:5 says, "Who is this coming out of the wilderness, leaning upon her beloved? Who is this strong as the sun, fair as the moon, brilliant as the stars, and as awesome as an army with identity?" (see Song of Solomon 6:10). The Church is about to be changed from a "what" to a "who."

September 11, 2001, apparently changed us from a "what" to a "who." The entire world was asking, "Who has the answer?" and the Church was brought out of the corner of the field to the center of the field. On September 11th I received calls from world diplomats and from people all over the world asking, "Is there a word from God?" Do you remember that they were going to have a prayer with the President and Billy Graham with all those people? They called me and asked, "Has God spoken?" I said. "Yes He has." "Would you give us a word to read on the prayer ground?" I said, "Yes I will. It's Isaiah 26:3-4: **"Thou will keep him in perfect peace, whose mind is stayed on thee: because he trusteth in thee. Trust ye in the LORD forever: for in the LORD JEHOVAH is everlasting strength."** The Church will be brought from the corners to the center.

The world thought Wall Street would have the answer, and if Wall Street didn't then the Pentagon would. What was struck by the terrorists on September 11, 2001? Money and might were hit. Those are the two things that we have put our confidence in. We can get an attitude, "well we will survive and build another tower" and He will shake it down too. Some said, "Do you think this is really judgment

45

from God?" Why wouldn't it be? Do you think we are such a Holy nation? Do you think we don't deserve wrath? What we received was mercy.

God really gave us what we asked for. We have been telling Him to get out of the schools and out of the government for twenty odd years. He said okay. He gave us what we asked for. We asked Him to get out and He got out. Do you believe that if we keep asking Him, He'll give us what we want even if it is to our own demise? "I want quail, I want meat." He said, "Okay!" Then they died with it lodged between their teeth (see Numbers 11:33).

Do you know what I find now? You can pray in school—I don't see such a big gap now between Church and State. They are praying in government. You ask, "Was it judgment?" No!—He just pulled His hand back a little and withdrew His protection. We'll know when judgment comes. But, if this one doesn't wake us up, the next one will. This idea is over of thinking we will pray a little while and get a little serious—and then backslide. We are going to find out that we are either for Him or very much against Him. We are in desperate times.

So, back to Boaz. He rides up and asks, **"...Whose damsel is this?" (Ruth 2:5).** He brings her over and begins to talk to her.

> **And the servant that was set over the reapers answered and said, It is the Moabitish damsel that came back with Naomi out of the country of Moab:**
>
> **And she said, I pray you, let me glean and gather after the reapers among the sheaves: so**

she came, and hath continued even from the morning until now, that she tarried a little in the house.

Then said Boaz unto Ruth, Hearest thou not, my daughter? Go not to glean in another field, neither go from here, but abide here fast by my maidens. (Ruth 2:6-8).

Here is the Lord of the harvest telling Ruth to stay in his field and to stay near his maidens where she will feel safe and thereby welcoming her. I would suggest that the Church needs to heed this; we need to get in the harvest field of the Lord and abide near His servants. We need to get in the place where we are going to be fruitful.

Let thine eyes be on the field that they do reap, and go thou after them: have I not charged the young men that they shall not touch thee? and when thou art athirst, go unto the vessels, and drink of that which the young men have drawn (Ruth 2:9).

In this manner, Boaz provided protection and provision for her. When we get in the right place, God does the same for us. We get in the right place by faith and by taking action, just as Ruth did.

Then she fell on her face, and bowed herself to the ground, and said unto him, Why have I found grace in thine eyes, that thou shouldest take knowledge of me, seeing I am a stranger? (Ruth 2:10).

I love what she says in verse 10. "How did I find such favor?" She found it because she believed and proclaimed it. Then Boaz talks to her about her reputation before the Lord.

> **And Boaz answered and said unto her, It has fully been shewed me, all that thou hast done unto thy mother-in-law since the death of thine husband: and how thou hast left thy father and thy mother, and the land of thy nativity, and art come unto a people which thou knewest not heretofore.**
>
> **The LORD recompense thy work, and a full reward be given thee of the LORD God of Israel, under whose wings thou art come to trust (Ruth 2:11-12).**

We learn several things from these verses. He had already done some research on her and he says, **"...It has fully been shewed me..."** How many of us believe everything in our life has been fully shown to God? In the His eyes we are all naked and exposed. There is not one thought in our mind that has not been fully made known to Him. We need to understand that there is nothing in our life, that has not been fully made known to the Lord. It is amazing that He knows all about us and yet, He still loves us.

We also learn that Boaz understood that Ruth trusted the Lord, not him (see Ruth 2:12). This is a very important lesson for us to learn: we must focus on the Source, not the resource. Many people in the Church put their eyes on the resource and not the Source. Let me give you an example: A wealthy person moves into a church, and they are a lovely child of God and they love to give. It is in their heart to give, and they begin to give a lot over a period of time. If you are not very careful, you will begin to look to the resource, instead of the Source. When this happens, God will have to remove the resource because you are putting your trust in the resource while neglecting God. Therefore, we see Boaz first lays the foundation for Ruth by telling her that he knows that it was **"...the LORD God of Israel, under whose wings thou art come to trust" (Ruth 2:12).**

As a preacher, I really appreciate it when people are looking to the Lord instead of to me. The Lord's behavior is not like ours or that of our friends, when upon learning a few negative things about one another will often become distant. But "the friend that sticks closer than a brother" is not like that, is He? When He finds out that we are hurting, He comes to help. He does not distance Himself, He draws near. He is a very present help in the time of trouble.

> **Then she said, Let me find favour in thy sight, my lord; for thou hast comforted me, and for that thou hast spoken friendly unto thine handmaid, though I be not like unto one of thine handmaidens (Ruth 2:13).**

She lets him know that she feels safe with him and that she realizes he knows she is different than the other girls.

Then he begins to say to her all he is going to do for her. He instructs his young men in the fields to provide bread and drink for her and not to touch her in an ungodly manner. He begins to tell her to follow and stay in "his harvest field" and not to go to another field. He tells her to stay near his reapers and he tells them to tend to her. He tells her in verse 14 that they will bring her bread to eat and that she can dip her bread in vinegar to add flavor to the meal. He was telling her that she could find sustenance in his harvest field. I want to say to the Church that this is so true: The place we can find nourishment to keep us going during the harvest time is in His harvest field.

And Boaz said unto her, At mealtime come thou hither, and eat of the bread, and dip thy morsel in the vinegar. And she sat beside the reapers: and he reached her parched corn, and she did eat, and was sufficed, and left (Ruth 2:14).

He served her roasted (parched) corn, which was carefully prepared food for her. She ate it until she was full and still had some left for later. He was demonstrating his love for her by serving her food he prepared for her when it was her place to serve him. These verses are telling us that he already knew her and he already loved her.

And when she was risen up to glean, Boaz commanded his young men, saying, Let her glean even among the sheaves, and reproach her not: (Ruth 2:15).

Isn't it something how God will make a way when it seems there is no way? He brought her out of a pagan place, out of the corner of the field and now she is in the center of the field where the very harvest sheaves are, where the big heart of the grain is. And, the owner of the field is saying, "Don't reproach or rebuke her, don't insult her or ridicule her, let her have all she can gather." Then he goes even further in blessing her in the next verse.

Handfuls of Purpose

And let fall also some of the handfuls of purpose for her, and leave them, that she may glean them, and rebuke her not (Ruth 2:16).

This verse is so wonderful. Again, remember that Boaz is a "type" of Jesus, and the reapers are a "type" of the angels. Boaz tells the reapers to leave her "handfuls of purpose." When Boaz gets involved, God is going to bring abundance. When Boaz gets involved, Ruth comes out of the corner of the field, out of just picking up leftovers, to what? Handfuls! I want you to understand that it is God's will for you to have handfuls. You may want to live in poverty but it's not the will of God. It's the will of God to bring you out of the corner to a place of handfuls. This sounds like the Church has a destiny. We are not going to fizzle out in the end. God is laying out, by His divine angels, handfuls of opportunity. It's time to lay hold of what God is laying out for us.

We, as the Church, have been off in the wilderness. We've been down in Moab, the country where they conceive by incestuous living. You know we have been friends with the world. But God is calling us out of that. Now He's calling us to a place where there'll be a field that we can get in.

Who are these reapers? Have you ever studied what Jesus said about the reapers? They're the angels, according to Jesus. When we get into God's field, His servants come along to help us. They'll start leaving us handfuls. Many Christians know just enough to "get by." You can live in the corner of a field if you want. You *can* stay down there in death and destruction if you want, but God is bringing us out! God is bringing us out and, in this sense, I believe Naomi was a "type" of the Holy Spirit saying, "There's a better life than this. Come on, let's get out of this old land, and back to where we belong."

Shared Blessings

So she gleaned in the field until even, and beat out what she had gleaned: and it was about an ephah of barley.

And she took it up, and went into the city: and her mother-in-law saw what she had gleaned: and she brought forth and gave to her that she had reserved after she was sufficed.

And her mother-in-law said unto her, Where hast thou gleaned today? and where wroughtest thou? blessed be he that did take knowledge of thee. And she shewed her mother-in-law with whom she had wrought, and said, The man's name with whom I wrought today is Boaz.

And Naomi said unto her daughter-in-law, Blessed be he of the LORD, who hath not left off his kindness to the living and to the dead. And Naomi said unto her, The man is near of kin unto us, one of our next kinsmen (Ruth 2: 17-20).

Ruth gleans in the field until evening, then beats out the barley, and she carries it to her mother-in-law. Naomi says, "Good God girl, where have you been?" And Ruth replies, "You're not going to believe it Mama. I wound up in a field and this handsome man rode up and his name was Boaz." Naomi says, "Boaz! Why he's the only one that can meet all of our needs."

She was blessing the Lord for not leaving them without a kinsman-redeemer. She was talking about how Boaz can redeem all the things that need to be redeemed.

> **And Ruth, the Moabitess said, He said unto me also, Thou shalt keep fast by my young men, until they have ended all my harvest (Ruth 2:21).**

How much of the harvest did Boaz tell her to stay through? **"all my harvest."** We find out later that she also stays through the corn harvest.

> **And Naomi said unto Ruth her daughter-in-law, It is good, my daughter, that thou go out with his maidens, that they meet thee not in any other field (Ruth 2:22).**

"...It is good..." "It's a fine thing; it's a good thing!" Naomi, as a "type" of the Holy Spirit, is always on a mission to get Ruth closer to Boaz, the "redeemer." Do you see that? There is this wonderful, driving dynamic about Naomi, and that is to get Ruth more intimate with Boaz.

The Meaning of Kinsman-Redeemer

The words of this old song are timeless: "Redeemed—how I love to proclaim it! Redeemed by the blood of the

Lamb; Redeemed by His infinite mercy, His child and forever, I am."

"...The man is near of kin unto us, one of our next kinsmen" (Ruth 2:20). Other versions variously translate "next kinsmen" as family redeemers, kinsman-redeemers and closest relatives. The word literally means, "redeemer" and is from the Hebrew word "ga´al." The Book of Ruth is a beautiful account of the kinsman-redeemer. His responsibility is summed up in the following verse.

> **What day thou buyest the field of the hand of Naomi, thou must buy it also of Ruth the Moabitess, the wife of the dead, to raise up the name of the dead upon his inheritance (Ruth 4:5).**

Thus the kinsman-redeemer was responsible for preserving the integrity, life, and property of their relative, as well as his family name. This was done through marriage and child bearing.

The word "redeemed" is connected with the laws of the firstborn. As a reminder of slaying all the Egyptian firstborn but sparing the Israelites, God retained an eternal claim on the life of all Israelite firstborn males, both of men and of cattle. The cattle were often sacrificed, **"...but all the firstborn of my children I redeem" (Exodus 13:15).**

The people of God later confessed, **"Thou in thy mercy hast led forth the people which thou hast redeemed..." (Exodus 15:13).**

God stated about Himself, "...**I am the Lord, and I will redeem you with an stretched out arm..." (Exodus 6:6)**.

The Psalmist tells us, **"Thou hast with thine arm redeemed thy people..." (Psalms 77:15).**

In the Book of Isaiah we find the word "ga´al" used to evidence the word "redeemed." It was used eleven times between chapters 35 and 63.

The word "redeemer," also translated from the word "ga´al" was used thirteen times of God, first in Isaiah 43:1, **"...Fear not; for I have redeemed thee, I have called thee by thy name; thou art mine."**

God also names Himself "redeemer," **"Thus saith the LORD, your Redeemer, the Holy One of Israel..." (Isaiah 43:14).**

> **And they remembered that God was their rock, And the Most High God their Redeemer (Psalms 78:35 NAS).**

In Psalms 103:2 and 4, we are told to, **"Bless the LORD, O my soul, and forget not all his benefits,...Who redeemeth thy life from destruction; who crowneth thee with lovingkindness and tender mercies."** We must never forget that we have been redeemed with the precious blood of Jesus Christ.

Where Is the Church Headed?

The Church has now been brought out of the land of loose living and from the corner of the field to the center of the field. Notice this as well: As Ruth is brought out, her boundaries get narrower but her authority gets larger. She is brought from a country to a city, from a city to a field, and we are going to find out where she goes beyond that field.

Would you like to know where the Lord wants to bring the Church? If I had but one word to share with the Body of Christ right now, it is Ruth, Chapter 3. The Lord is saying, "Meet me tonight at the threshing floor." We have been so deluded and deceived that we thought we could meet Him at the "throne floor." He wants our faith at His feet at the threshing floor.

Naomi, who is a true "type" of the Holy Spirit, is going to tell Ruth how to prepare herself to have this engagement with the Lord at the threshing floor. You pastors and leaders need to study the threshing floor. Every time you find "threshing floor" in the Scriptures, you find God's people coming into a deeper intimacy with Him. What happens at the threshing floor? Separation takes place and the husk, the counterfeit, the fluff and that which is not the heart of the matter is separated.

Aren't you glad we are out of the land of loose living? I am aggravated at Elimelech for leading them down to Moab. He represents people who claim they know Him, but they really don't. We had better watch out when the blind are leading the blind or we will all end up stumbling.

I believe we have been lingering for too long in the land of leftovers. Aren't you tired of living off of past anointings? Aren't you tired of living off of what others have touched, dropped, and discarded? Scavenging off of what other people mishandled? I am tired of living that way.

The Lord is bringing us out of the corner of the field to the center of the field. At the center of the field we will find purpose. We will find an engagement with Boaz, but the ultimate result is something else. Remember we started this story in Ruth 4:13 where we learn that Boaz married Ruth, went into Ruth and impregnated her, and she had a baby. They took the baby out of the arms of Ruth and brought the baby to Naomi. From that moment on the baby was known as Naomi's. We are going to find out that we will willingly give any fruit we may have back to the One from whom it came. We are going to lay any crown we may receive back at the feet of the One to whom it belongs.

There is hidden truth in the Book of Ruth that will blow your mind. It is a prophetic message to the Church. Aren't you ashamed that we have had such an arrogant attitude about ourselves, that we have believed that we could sashay into His presence and say, "Hey! I am the one you've been waiting for buddy, look at me." Well you had better read Ruth chapter 3 again.

The prophetic message is that the Scriptures tell us that Boaz lay down at midnight. Midnight is the darkest hour of the night. It is when the sun is the greatest distance from setting and the greatest distance from rising. This is where we are right now; in the darkest hour. But we will find that if we come to Him and snuggle at His feet, as a willing bride made ready, then things will change very quickly for us. It says in Ruth 3:9 that at midnight he was startled and asked, "Who is this at my feet." She said, "I am Ruth, your handmaiden. Cover your skirt over me." Her will and her womb were open to him. Did he want to be with her? Does Jesus want to consummate this thing called the Church? And, he said, "Oh, I want to, but, there is one standing in the way."

Now, this is a strange thing. We think we know so much, but look. Naomi says, "Meet him at the threshing floor." She meets him at the threshing floor and she is snuggled at his feet. Her desire is for his skirt to come over her, for him to impregnate her, to become one with him. And he says, "I want to; however, there is one standing in the way." You see, the Lord will not do the right thing in the wrong way. Everyone else in this story is named except this one man. In Ruth 4:1 he is called, **"such a one"** or "old so and so." I know who he is, he is the one who has been lurking in the shadows, preventing this union from happening, which is why we have got to have government in the house.

Ruth goes from a country—Moab, to a city— Bethlehem. Then she goes from a city to a field, from a field to a floor, and from a floor to a gate. The next move of God is going to bring government into the house. God is going to deal with this old **"such a one."** He will deal with whoever is standing in the way, preventing Boaz from knowing Ruth. Don't you want to know who it is? I want you to know who it is!

Examine Yourself

We must ask God if there is any part of Moab left in us. We certainly don't want to be like Lot's wife; starting out, but never making it to the top—turned back and rendered worthless.

Don't you think we've played around long enough? Don't you think we've tried to walk two paths long enough? You see, **"A double-minded man is unstable in all his ways" (James 1:8).**

When I was in Europe sometime ago I met a man who was a prominent minister there. He had attempted to murder a royal official and he was put into an insane asylum. The preacher I was traveling with had arranged for me to meet with this man and I told him I would do it. They got him out of the asylum and carried him to his home for me to meet him. We went into this deranged man's house and he sat at the end of his table all curled up in the fetus position. The insane minister's wife, the preacher who had invited me, and I sat at the table with him. I was sitting at the end of the table as I was just a guest there. The pastor and the insane minister's wife were discussing the garden and they were talking about the government—just a lot of small talk. The insane minister was manifesting terribly while they are chattering away. Finally the preacher turned to me and said, "Well Brother Bobby, did the Lord show you anything?"

I said, "Oh yes He did, the reason he is like this is because he is addicted to pornography." The wife kicked over her chair and jumped up and began to scream, "I did not tell him, I did not tell him!"

You see, the Bible tells us that, **"A double-minded man is unstable in all his ways."** In the attic of his house this prominent religious leader had all kinds of pornography and all kinds of seductive things. He would play his religious games and then he would play his pornography games. A double-minded man gets more and more unstable in all of his ways. I told them that pornography was the problem. I said that if you want to be clean from it, God will set you free. I'll never forget this, we cast the devil out of this man and it went out through the window. A dog that was sitting outside in the flower garden began to howl and howl because it had seen the evil spirit go out.

The formerly insane minister came to the church the next night and sat down on the front row. He was totally sane—totally healed.

I am quite sure that Elimelech never dreamed what the lifestyle was like when he went down to Moab. None of us would make a conscious choice to lead our families down into a degrading place. We drift away slowly. It is time to let God right the ship again in order to get us back on the straight and narrow way that leads to life. It is time for us to examine ourselves against the Word of God, repent of our sins, and to return to our Holy God.

The Bible tells us that, "**If I regard iniquity in my heart, the Lord will not hear me**" **(Psalms 66:18).** That's what He meant when He said, **"Your iniquities have separated between you and your God…" (Isaiah 59:2).** Do not regard iniquity in your heart. The word "regard" means to give it a safe place. It is the same thing that a woman's body does for a fetus—it gives it a safe nurturing place. Do not regard iniquity or give it a any place.

There is more for us than what we have been experiencing. Our destiny is to make Him known. When Jesus was praying to His Father he said, **"I have manifested thy name unto the men…"(John 17:6)** When I read that, the Lord said, "This sums up all of Christianity."

The Father chose to name Himself nine covenant names in the Old Testament. Then Jesus Christ came and gave flesh, form, and function to every one of those nine covenant names. Our job is to become a manifestation of

Him. That's why we must become intimate with Him; we must become like Him so that we can make His name known.

Chapter Three

Preparation

In this chapter, Naomi instructs Ruth on how to prepare her heart to go to meet the lord of the harvest. How does this chapter start? **"Then..."** What if Ruth had just sat under a tree somewhere when she got out of Moab instead of taking action as she did? Suppose for a moment that she had said, "Now, I know I'm a woman of destiny. I am going to just sit here until Boaz rides up and tells me that he's been waiting for me." Many people think that they have an awesome anointing, so they are just waiting for a great big door to swing wide open so they can walk out on the stage and proclaim themselves. Chances are that probably is not going to happen. If you are not faithful over a little, you can forget about ruling over a lot.

Ruth was faithful to glean in the corner of the field, then she was faithful to glean in the center of the field, and faithfulness will always lead to more. It is required of a steward to be found faithful. I know many people that have a genuine anointing, but they have a grandiose idea that TBN is going to come and sign them up. They will say that they can't go witness at the mall because TBN is coming, or "I've been promised nations, hallelujah; I can't go to the nursing homes." NATIONS!? Well forget about going to the nations until you can go to the nursing homes. He said, "If you've done it unto the least of these, you've done it unto Me." Are you waiting for a big time ministry? Find the hurting and helpless and then you'll be ministering to Him, and when you are ministering to Him—He opens doors for you.

Ruth was doing what was set before her. As she was faithful to do that, much more was set before her. That's why it says, **"Then…"**

> **Then Naomi her mother-in-law said unto her, My daughter, shall I not seek rest for thee, that it may be well with thee? And now is not Boaz of our kindred, with whose maidens thou wast? Behold, he winnoweth barley tonight in the threshing floor (Ruth 3:1-2).**

This is so important. It's the Holy Spirit reassuring Ruth that He has her best intention in mind. He's looking out for her. And, it's Naomi telling the Church where she can meet the Lord tonight.

Wash Yourself and Get Down

Here is the advice of Naomi, "the Holy Spirit" to the Church, **"Wash thyself…" (Ruth 3:2).** Here we have the Holy Spirit telling the Church how to get ready. Will we do that, will we prepare ourselves for Him? **"Let us rejoice and be glad and give the glory to Him, for the**

marriage of the Lamb has come *and His bride has made herself ready*" **(Revelation 19:7 NAS emphasis mine).**

Is it important to wash yourself? Ecclesiastes 9:8 tells us, "Let thy garments be always white; and let thy head lack no anointing" (paraphrase). Make sure your garments are always white. Do you remember when God was going to come and speak corporately to the people of Israel the first time on Mount Sinai? He told Moses in Exodus 19:10 to, **"have the people wash their clothes."** Psalms 24:3-4 asks, **"Who shall ascend into the hill of the LORD? He that hath clean hands, and a pure heart..."** Do you see through the words **"Wash thy self,"** that the Lord is telling us there needs to be preparation? We need to ask Him to **"Search me, O God, and know my heart: try me, and know my thoughts; and see if there be any wicked way in me, and lead me in the way everlasting" (Psalms 139:23-24).** Hebrews 10:22 tells us we need to be washed with pure water. What does water represent? The Word of God. If we are going to draw near to Him, we are going to have to draw near to His Word. This is referred to as the "washing of the water of the Word." Isaiah 1:16 tells us to wash and make ourselves clean. Jeremiah 4:14 speaks of washing your heart from wickedness. The prayer we need to pray is found in the Psalms: **"Purge me with hyssop, and I shall be clean: wash me, and I shall be whiter than snow" (Psalms 51:7).** This is all necessary if we are going to meet Him at the threshing floor: **"Create in me a clean heart, O God; and renew a right spirit within me" (Psalms 51:10).**

We have had much presumption in our hearts. We have thought we would have a face-to-face encounter with Him.

No, God wants a face-to-feet encounter. He wants us to put our face at His feet and then wait for Him to tell us what to do. We have been pressing in and trying to get our face in His face and then trying to tell Him what we want Him to do. We are way out of balance in this for God really is calling for a face to feet encounter.

> **Wash thy self therefore, and anoint thee, and put thy raiment upon thee, and get thee down to the floor: but make not thyself known unto the man, until he shall have done eating and drinking.**

> **And it shall be, when he lieth down, that thou shalt mark the place where he shall lie, and thou shalt go in, and uncover his feet, and lay thee down; and he will tell thee what thou shalt do (Ruth 3:3-4).**

He will tell us what to do instead of us trying to tell Him what to do in order to advance "our" ministry. Here we have the Church, curled at His feet, waiting for Him to give instruction.

Wash yourself, anoint yourself, listen to what the Holy Ghost says to you, and obey what the Lord says to you. And, it says, she did *all* she was instructed to do. If we could get to that point, we would be so much nearer to intimacy and so much nearer to revival.

That is what Naomi told Ruth. What if Ruth says, "Ha! I guess you just don't know who I am! I'm the gal out of Moab." I have counseled a lot of people and told them what God says to do and they reply, "Ha! I guess you don't know who I am! Do you think I'm going to do that?"

Naaman Gets Down

Do you remember Naaman the king who was a leper? The prophet sent his servant and told him to wash in the muddy Jordan seven times and Naaman went into a rage (see II Kings 5:1-14). "Who does he think I am? Doesn't he know that I have power, and prestige, and pomp?" "Yeah, and you've got leprosy too!" You see, God has a way of bringing the "high" down. He also has a way of bringing those who are "down" up.

So Naaman the leper is in a rage and would have died with leprosy, if it had not been for one of his servants. He stomps off, and tells everyone that the prophet must not know who he is. He thought Elisha would come out and make a big production and then tell him to do something extraordinary. He thought he should call a big conference, get TBN to air it, get Benny Hinn and a bunch of guys out there and make a really big deal out of it. After all, here is a pagan man who is about to come into the Kingdom. But Naaman stomps off, dying in his leprosy, and falling apart at the seams, literally. That's how someone with leprosy dies, isn't it? He was beside himself, and without a leg to stand on—powerless. In his rotten rage, his servant says, "**... if the prophet had bid thee do some great thing, wouldest thou not have done it? How much rather then, when he saith to thee, wash, and be clean?" (II Kings 5:13).** He must have agreed because he went down to the muddy Jordon "**...then he went down, and dipped himself seven times...**" and guess what happened? On the seventh time, he came up and the Bible says that his flesh was like that of a little baby. He was brand new. When you obey God, you get God's provision.

Ruth's Obedience

Look at what Ruth says to Naomi.

> **And she said unto her, All that thou sayest unto me I will do.**
>
> **And she went down unto the floor, and did according to all that her mother-in-law bade her (Ruth 3:5-6).**

Have you ever wondered why Acts 2:1 says, **"...they were all with one accord in one place."** This is very important. Why were they in that place? Here is where we can learn why many people are not in the anointing; it is because they are not in the right place. The disciples were in that place because of Luke 24:49. God instructs them to, **"...tarry in Jerusalem..."** the right place **"...until ye be endued with power from on high."** What if they had said, "We don't like Jerusalem this time of year; much too much camel." I have actually heard similar excuses as to why we can't follow God, such as: "Music's too loud, pews are too soft, or have you seen that music director's hair?" It is always, "we can't follow God because of this or that." But the disciples did what they were told to do and they got what God promised to give. The Holy Ghost is given to those who obey. You have to obey as Ruth obeyed and she did **"all"** Naomi told her to do.

The Double Portion

> **And when Boaz had eaten and drunk, and his heart was merry, he went to lie down at the end of the heap of corn; and she came softly, and uncovered his feet, and laid her down.**

And it came to pass at midnight, that the man was affraid, and turned himself: and, behold, a woman lay at his feet.

And he said, Who art thou? And she answered, I am Ruth thine handmaid: spread therefore thy skirt over thine handmaid; for thou art a near kinsman (Ruth 3:7-9).

Once again, we have wanted a face-to-face encounter with God when He is asking us to put our face humbly at His feet. God is calling the Church to the threshing floor which is the place of being broken and empty. It is time for the Church to get down to the true heart of the matter.

Notice how Ruth came quietly and with humility to the threshing floor. It is not a time to attempt to proudly push into His presence. We cannot come in proudly and with arrogance.

Ruth's actions were not at all out of line, and there is not the faintest touch of impurity about it. The Spirit of God had obviously instructed Ruth, through Naomi, for the Mosaic Law states:

If brethren dwell together, and one of them die, and have no child, the wife of the dead shall not marry without unto a stranger: her husband's brother shall go in unto her, and take her to him to wife, and perform the duty of an husband's brother unto her. And it shall be, that the first-born which she beareth shall succeed in the name of his brother which is dead, that his name be not put out of Israel (Deuteronomy 25:5-6).

Suddenly, around midnight Boaz is awakened and startled—there was a woman lying at his feet! The midnight hour is the darkest hour and the farthest from sunset and sunrise. It was at midnight, while imprisoned, that Paul and Silas sang praises unto God (see Acts 16:25). We are also living in dark days; however, we can gain confidence and courage that our heavenly Boaz is about to stir Himself. We will do well to be at His feet waiting on His command.

"Who are you?" he demanded. This question is about to resound across the entire earth, "Who is this at the feet of Christ?" Who is the Church? The answer is found in Song of Solomon: **"Who is this that grows like the dawn, as beautiful as the full moon, as pure as the sun, as awesome as an army with banners?" (Song of Solomon 6:10)**

"Who are you?" Boaz asked. "Master, it is I—Ruth." she replied. "Make me your wife according to God's law, for you are my close relative."

Ruth is saying to Boaz that her will and her womb were open to him. "Do unto me anything you want." This is the same heart Mary had when she said, **"...be it unto me according unto thy word..." (Luke 1:38).**

> **And he said, Blessed be thou of the LORD, my daughter: for thou hast shewed more kindness in the latter end than at the beginning, inasmuch as thou followedst not young men, whether poor or rich.**
>
> **And now, my daughter, fear not; I will do to thee all that thou requirest: for all the city of**

my people doth know that thou art a virtuous woman (Ruth 3:10-11).

Basically Boaz said, "Thank God for a girl like you! You are being even kinder to Naomi now than before. Naturally you would prefer a younger man, even though poor. But you have put aside your personal desires. Now don't worry about a thing, my child; I will handle all the details, for everyone knows what a wonderful person you are."

And now it is true that I am thy near kinsman: howbeit, there is a kinsman nearer than I.

Tarry this night, and it shall be in the morning, that if he will perform unto thee the part of a kinsman, well; let him do the kinsman's part: but if he will not do the part of a kinsman to thee, then will I do the part of a kinsman to thee, as the LORD liveth: lie down until the morning (Ruth 3:12-13).

But what does he do? He doesn't touch her. You see, he will not do the right thing in the wrong way. He doesn't violate her because he won't do the right thing out of order. There was one more person standing in line that superceded his right to redeem her.

And she lay at his feet until the morning: and she rose up before one could know another. And he said, Let it not be known that a woman came into the floor.

Also he said, Bring the veil that thou hast upon thee, and hold it. And when she held it, he

measured six measures of barley, and laid it on her: and she went into the city (Ruth 3:14-15).

In verse 15, he asked her to bring him her veil—the Hebrew word is "mantel." "Bring me your veil, your mantel." You never come to Him and go away empty handed. You will never come and snuggle at His feet, draw near to Him, and then go away empty handed. So, he calls her just as she's going back to her mother-in-law and as she is about to leave the threshing floor. He says, "Wait! Bring me your mantel you have upon you." And he measured out six measures of barley. When she worked, she only got three. Do you see that when we come to Him, He doubles what He gives? Do you see that? We are in the end-time and we receive the double anointing. When she worked all she could get for her efforts was half of what he freely gave her. But now she has come to him, and all she has do is lay at his feet—more can be done near Him than laboring on your own.

And when she came to her mother-in-law, she said, Who art thou, my daughter? And she told her all that the man had done to her.

And she said, These six measures of barley gave he me; for he said to me, Go not empty unto thy mother-in-law (Ruth 3:16-17).

Boaz gives her six measures and lays the grain upon her and she goes back into the city. He had told her to give the grain to her mother-in-law and Ruth completed her obedience by giving the grain to Naomi.

Then said she, Sit still, my daughter, until thou know how the matter will fall: for the man

will not be in rest, until he have finished the thing this day (Ruth 3:18).

And Naomi says, "Be still, he's not going to rest until this thing is finished this day" (see Ruth 3:18). **"this day"** is very important.

Do you believe we are in **"this day"** spoken about in Ruth 3:18? God has called us to the floor. What is going to take place at the threshing floor? Every time you find the "threshing floor" in the Bible, you find an encounter between God and His people. Many outstanding events have occurred at the threshing floor, for this is where the real heart of the matter is exposed. All the fluff and exterior is removed. This is a place where the counterfeit is exposed and the real is brought forth.

Listen to what John the Baptist had to say about the threshing floor. **"And His winnowing fork is in His hand, and He will thoroughly clear His threshing floor; and He will gather His wheat into the barn, but He will burn up the chaff with unquenchable fire" (Matthew 3:12 NAS).** You see, you don't stay at the threshing floor; it's a place of separation. You go to the barn or to the fire.

Gideon tested God at the threshing floor. David stopped the plague at a threshing floor. Uzzah died at the threshing floor of Nachon (see II Samuel 6:6-7). Uzzah's name means. "my strength." When you try to touch God's work with your strength, somebody has to decline and it will not be God. He tried to steady the ark of God. Why did he get into trouble there? He got into trouble because David tried to bring the ark in on a new cart. The Lord never said to carry the ark on a cart, it was to be borne on the shoulders of the anointed ones. David got the idea to move the ark that way; from the Philistines. You see, you cannot take the ways of the world and win the Kingdom.

We need to understand the word of the Lord: **"...come out from among them, and be ye separate, says the LORD..." (see II Corinthians 6:17)**. Many people see how close they can walk to the world thinking they are going to win the world, but that is not what the Bible teaches. You don't bring light by becoming dark. You bring light by being light. So, David tried to bring the ark in on a new cart. They got to a threshing floor and it almost toppled over. Then a man, in his own strength, reached out—and, it says that the anger of the Lord burned against him and he died.

The real us is exposed when we come to a threshing floor. One of the first open visions I had, that I shared publicly, was about a threshing floor. Winnowing, sifting wheat, throwing away the chaff and keeping the good. Do you remember where He says He's winnowing? At the threshing floor. What does that mean; winnowing? They take a big, three pronged fork, stick it into the stubble and toss it into the air. The wind blows the chaff away and the grain (good fruit) settles to the floor. They do it again and again and again. Have you ever felt like you don't know which end is up? Well, welcome to the threshing floor.

Another way that they separated the grain from the husk was to let a big animal walk on it, and sometimes they used a big grinding rock. You might say, "I don't know why I'm going through this pressure." Welcome to the threshing floor.

Grain is not much good when it's just in the field or in the barn. It needs to be eaten or planted. That's the only reason we have grain. We don't say, "look at all my barley" and then just sit around looking at it. No, it's good for only two things to serve its purpose—grinding to eat or for planting to produce good fruit. That's the only reason we have grain—nourishment for others. You see, if we've come to a place where we are just worshiping the grain, we have perverted our purpose and prevented our progress. If that's what we are doing by just sitting in a church, then we are worshiping something else and not God, and we are not doing what He is telling us to do.

The Word of God

We need to be very careful here. Our enemy has many plans and schemes for our destruction. When you are a prophetic person, you must be very careful not to get into the second heaven and prophesy openly the devils plans. If you do, it can help them come to pass. What you should do is find out what the enemy is going to do and counter-act those plans with proclamation.

What I do when facing this situation is speak the opposite of the devil's plans. If I learn that he is going to attack children and sports stadiums, I proclaim, "God is going to protect the children. He is protecting sports stadiums; He is an awesome protector." We are going to have to learn the Word of God like never before, so that when the enemy comes in, we can come back at him with the sword of the Spirit.

During all my years in ministry, I have seen the devil (personally) only twice. A lot of people say, "Oh man, I saw the devil…" I don't think so. If you think he is some grotesque, ugly thing, you've never seen him. He is the most handsome, persuasive being I have ever seen.

The last time I saw him was in a vision, and my friend Bob Jones and I were sitting in cane back chairs. There were people as far as you could see. There were multitudes of people and they were just drinking in every word we said. We were telling them prophetic truths and then—have you ever seen a tennis match when everyone's attention is diverted? I saw all the people's faces turn slowly in the same direction and there was a veil, like a curtain or a shroud, and something was behind the shroud. As I listened, the most flowery words that you have ever heard were coming from behind the shroud. I looked behind it, and there, sitting in an overstuffed leather chair, was the devil. He was dressed in a shining silk jacket that was very elegant. He was sitting there, not in straight cane back chairs, but very comfortable and relaxed. He looked over the people and said, "These men are exactly right. Everything they say to you is total truth." I thought, "What is this?" He was winning the people, winning their hearts with every word. Then he said, "What they say to you is absolutely true; but if you come to me, you can have all they have—without the cost." You see, people want that—they want all the power without the price. Can you see that this is why we must go down to the threshing floor? That is why witchcraft is so rampant in the Church. I said to Bob, "we'll never out-talk him." I knew we would never out-talk him. As I sat there watching the people being mused and deceived by him, a tap came on my shoulder. I turned and it was the Lord Jesus and He handed me a dagger. Bob Jones said, "Call it a sword." No, it was a

76

dagger and the Lord put it in my right hand. He said, "Go, take this dagger and put it in under his rib, through his lung and into his heart." That is when the vision ended.

The only weapon we have is the sword of the Spirit, which is the Word of God (see Ephesians 6:17) and that is what the dagger represented. The rib, lung, and heart in this vision were very important. Where was the Lord pierced and where did you (ladies) come from? The side, the rib. I will tell you that the *heart* of the matter is the Word of God and we will have to have it as an offensive weapon.

You can see that we must remain obedient to the Word of God, or we can be easily deceived. We must go through the experiences He has set before us and we must not turn away from the threshing floor. We must be obedient to do what He tells us, and to do it in His time—not ours.

Enter by the narrow gate; for wide is the gate and broad is the way that leads to destruction, and there are many who go in by it. Because narrow is the gate and difficult is the way, which leads unto life, and there are few who find it (Matthew 7:13-14 NKJV).

Boaz's Encounter With "Such A One"

Remember that Ruth has been brought from a country to a city, from a field to a floor, and now to a gate.

> **Then went Boaz up to the gate, and sat down there: and, behold, the kinsman of whom Boaz spake came by; unto whom he said, Ho, such a one! turn aside, sit down here. And he turned aside, and sat down (Ruth 4:1).**

I found something here that is very intriguing. Every person in this story has a name except for this guy called, "such a one." What is the deal with that? Elimelech had a name, Orpah has a name, Ruth has a name, Naomi has a name and the two boys that died were named. Why would this person, who seems to be so much a part of the story, be nameless? Why would God meticulously name everyone else in this story and then when we get to the main guy that is spoiling the plot—the main guy that's keeping an intimate relationship between the Church and Jesus from happening—why is he nameless? The King James says, **"such a one."** Basically it's, "Hey you!" One translation says "friend," but that's not what the Hebrew says. It basically says, "Hey you, come over here and sit down."

This thing they are about to talk about will be settled in the gate, which speaks of government. One of the reasons the Church is not having this intimate relationship with Jesus Christ, that God wants to give to us, is because there is no real government in the house. So, God is in the process of bringing government; He is bringing the Church from the threshing floor to the gate where He can put order into the house of God. Again, the word "gate" is speaking to us about government.

So, we have a man that is standing in the way between Boaz, the "strong, steadfast, sure one," and Ruth, the "warm, welcoming, cordial one," thereby keeping him from intimacy with her. Ruth is a "type" of the Church and Boaz is a "type" of Jesus, so who is this guy? When I read this story it leapt out at me. I said, "God! Who is he? I want to know who he is, and why you didn't give him a name!"

Many times, when something is very, very important, God will make you search it out. Do you remember that the Bible says, **"It is the glory of God to conceal a thing: but the honour of kings is to search out a matter" (Proverbs 25:2).** When it is a paramount issue, sometimes you have to look hard to find the answer.

Do you remember that God gave Moses very specific and detailed instructions on how to build every piece of furniture in the Tabernacle? However, there is one piece of furniture that He did not provide any dimensions for—the laver. Not one dimension was given for the laver. The laver was where you cleansed yourself. He did tell them to make it out of the looking glass, but why were no dimensions given? The answer is because we tend to become so mechanical and rigid. "Well, if I walk up six steps and I do this or that, then I'll have what I want." No, it is not going to be some legalistic thing that you can make into a formula and then you'll be okay. The laver— no real dimensions were given for that. A lot of people want the "seven steps to success." No, it's not that way.

We need to understand that "such a one" represents somebody. I know who he is. I know who the Lord said he is and I know he's called on every one of us. He is this old "such a one"— the guy that is standing in the way of an intimate relationship between Ruth and Boaz. Boaz wants her and she wants him, but Boaz will never do the right thing in the wrong way. Look at what happens.

They are sitting at the gate. Do you see how many people are sitting at the gate? We've got "such a one" and Boaz sitting there, and Boaz took ten men with him.

And he took ten men of the elders of the city, and said, Sit ye down here. And they sat down (Ruth 4:2).

That is a total of twelve people at the gate. Again, as with the gate, twelve is the number that represents government.

This is intriguing. This is the very guy that is standing in the way of Boaz knowing Ruth in a very, very intimate way. Listen to what Boaz says to "such a one."

And he said unto the kinsman, Naomi, that is come again out of the country of Moab,

selleth a parcel of land, which was our brother Elimelech's:

And I thought to advertise thee, saying, Buy it before the inhabitants, and before the elders of my people. If thou wilt redeem it, redeem it: but if thou wilt not redeem it, then tell me, that I may know: for there is none to redeem it beside thee; and I am after thee. And he said, I will redeem it (Ruth 4:3-4).

So, "such a one" says he wants to redeem the property. He jumps at the deal. He says, "Yeah, I want it!"

Then said Boaz, What day thou buyest the field of the hand of Naomi, thou must buy it also of Ruth, the Moabitess, the wife of the dead, to raise up the name of the dead upon his inheritance (Ruth 4:5).

In other words, Boaz said, "Oh, and by the way, when you take the parcel, you have to get involved with the person, you are going to have to have a relationship with Ruth."

And the kinsman said, I cannot redeem it for myself, lest I mar mine own inheritance: redeem thou my right to thyself; for I cannot redeem it (Ruth 4:6).

He tells Boaz, "You'll have to redeem it." Now, what is the deal here? Who is it that has wanted your possessions, but not your person? I'll tell you who it is—man-made religion. It is religion that comes from man's thoughts, ideas, and traditions but has nothing to do with a direct and intimate relationship with God. They want your stuff, but they don't want a relationship with you. They want your possessions, but not your person.

Did you notice that "such a one" jumped at the chance to have her possessions? "I'll do it, sign me up!" Then Boaz says, "Oh, and by the way, if you take her stuff, you'll have to enter into a relationship with her." We are about to find out that this whole thing is based upon relationship. I'll tell you that it will be shocking when we find out how many are not even saved because they have never had relationship with Jesus. Jesus said, "Depart from Me you workers of iniquity; I never had a relationship with you, I never knew you, I never was intimate with you, I never put Myself in you, I never became part of you" (see Matthew 7:23). Many people sign on the dotted line and they get either christened, sprinkled, confirmed, or they go through some ritual, but they don't have their own relationship with the Lord.

This guy right here, "such a one" is standing in the way of an intimate relationship between Jesus and the Church—he is man-made religion. But God is about to expose that and shake it down because government is going to demand accountability. If you take their stuff, you are going to have to get involved in their life. His government will expose religion and weed it out; very quickly. Do you remember when Jesus said, "Except you eat my flesh and drink My blood, you have no part in Me" (see John 6:53). A little further in John 6 it tells you the result: "And many followed Him no more" (see John 6:66). Do you see that it doesn't get any more governmental than Jesus? Remember the government rests on His shoulders" (see Isaiah 9:6). You might say, "Wow! I did not want to get involved, I just wanted the benefit. You would be surprised how many people are in Church just because they like the benefit, but they don't have time for the person.

We are seeing much the same results of man-made religion in our day. For example, some of these mega-ministries are just acquiring the substance of the people without accepting any real relationship to the people. Many ministries have fallen into this snare. The Spirit of God is seeking to bring to the forefront true relationship and personal encounters with people.

He Still Chooses the Common

One thing that has always aggravated me in our society is when somebody gets the least bit of anointing, or the least bit of recognition, then others begin to usher them in and out. "Back off, you're too close to the preacher!" Jesus was not that way—not at all. He was so accessible that even little children got in His lap. Now, I know there are all kinds of things you have to watch out for. But, this idea of thinking preachers are some kind of celebrities is...well, you finish the sentence. Through this idea we have sown into the hearts of Church leadership that the only kind of people God should give us are the big and famous ones. That is absolutely anti-scriptural. God uses ordinary people to do extraordinary things so that He gets the glory. It says in I Corinthians 1:26, **"For you see your calling, brethren, that not many wise according to the flesh, not many mighty, not many noble, are called"** **(NKJV).** He chooses the common. Do not buy into the lie that if you are not on TBN or not in Charisma Magazine, God probably will not be able to use you. The Kingdom of God is carried by unknown believers. We will be shocked to find that not many of the "big names" down here will be high up when they are in Heaven. Do you believe that God uses little, insignificant nobodies to catapult the Kingdom down the road? Oh yes, He does!

Unsung Heroes

Every one of us knows something about Paul the Apostle. He wrote the biggest part of the New Testament, and he started most of the New Testament churches. But he would have been killed if not for his nephew. When God showed me this, I didn't even know Paul had a sister or that she had a son. Paul would have been assassinated and died prematurely if it had not been for a little boy who was at the right place at the right time. Paul's sister's son overheard an assassination attempt being plotted against his uncle and spoiled it. You'll be surprised when we get to Heaven because that little boy is going to have just as much fruit as his uncle, Paul the Apostle. God uses insignificant people in little slices of their life to catapult the Kingdom down the road to fulfill His purposes. No one has ever heard a sermon on Paul's nephew. We can go to the bookstore and find volumes written about Paul, yet there is not one single message on his nephew.

Ananias

Remember when God was ready to initiate the call of Saul of Tarsus, who later became Paul, into the ministry? Who did He call on? An unknown disciple from Damascus, named Ananias. There are not volumes of books written about Ananias. He never called down fire from Heaven, nor had he done great and mighty deeds. But when the Son of God got ready to commission His greatest warrior in the New Testament, the Lord said, **"And there was a certain disciple at Damascus, named Ananias" (Acts 9:10)**. The Lord came to Ananias and said, **"Ananias."** Here is his response to the Lord: **"Behold, I am here LORD."** Do you see the relationship and faithful communion in this? Those who are faithful over a little get to rule over much. Wouldn't you like to be the guy who initiated the ministry of Paul, the Apostle? Nobody had ever heard of Ananias—except for God. He is truly one of the unsung heroes of the New Testament. We must stop thinking that we have to be the rich and famous or God will not use us.

Ananias said "yes" to the Lord. His response was not, "Huh? Who was that?" He knew Him because he had daily fellowship with Him.

The Lord told Ananias, "I want you to go to a street called Straight, and there is a fellow down there and his name is Saul of Tarsus. He is praying. I want you to go in and lay hands on him to commission him for the service for which I have called him that he might receive his sight." (see Acts 9:10-11).

I want you to understand that Ananias was not out of the loop; he was aware of what had been going on with Saul. If you study about Ananias, he said, "Well Lord, I understand this guy is extremely hostile to the Church" (see Acts 9:13-14). Ananias was not out of the loop—he knew what was going on. Many people think that if you are an intercessor you must get away on a rock somewhere and dance around and pray loudly in tongues while staying out of the loop. No, that's not right, because you need to be, and had better be, informed. Ananias was not some weird guy that was out of the loop not knowing what was going on. When the Lord told him to go down to the street called Straight and lay hands on Saul, he began to talk to the Lord about the character of Saul. "I've heard this…, and I've heard that…" Can you see, he was not out of the loop? I believe that God can use you if you know more about what is going on.

Many people think that we, the Chruch, are just a bunch of nuts. They say, "Yuck, the Church. They don't know anything." They think of us like a mosquito bite—a little irritant they thought would go away. That's exactly what the world thinks about the Church—but they are finding out that the Church has answers.

So, the Lord tells Ananias to go lay hands on Saul and the first words out of his mouth are, **"Brother Saul…" (Acts 9:17). "Brother…"** That word represents total communion with Saul. Isn't that wonderful? Ananias is representative of the kind of people God can use. Those who do not continue to question what they think they see—they unashamedly follow and obey God.

I Never Signed Up For This

Now, we have Boaz and he has brought this nameless person, who is standing in the way, up to the place of government. Boaz and "such a one" are sitting at the gate with ten elders, totaling twelve people. Boaz tells him that he wants him to redeem the land and he says he will, but then Boaz tells him about the little string attached to the deal they are about to make. If he buys the land, he has to have a relationship with Ruth, the Moabitess. "Such a one" tells Boaz no, he won't take the land, because it will mess up what he already has going. Do you see that? It's in Ruth 4:6. The King James says, **"...lest I mar mine own inheritance...."**

You would be surprised, when God begins to check people's hearts, how often pastors will say, "Hey, I never signed up for this. It will mar what I have going on." Pastors you will be surprised how the Holy Ghost will mar what you have got going on. He loves to mess up the gig you've got going. Do you honestly think you are going to be able to get through this move of God with your superior attitude? I don't think so.

A friend of mine, Jack Deere wrote a book in which he mentioned a sermon preached by Paul Cain titled, *"The Anointing vs. Respectability."* You cannot have both of them. You cannot have the applause of men and the raw anointing of God. Every person who had the anointing in the New Testament was accused of being either demon possessed or a lunatic. Do you think you are any different? The servant is no greater than his master. The only reason we are sliding along so easily and getting away with so much is because we are not enough like Him yet. If we start living out who we really are, there will be a quick cutting away. We are blending in with the world way too much.

Seal the Deal

So, here is what happened. Boaz wanted her and took her for himself. They got the business settled by taking off their sandals.

**Therefore the kinsman said unto Boaz, Buy
it for thee. So he drew off his shoe (Ruth 4:8).**

In the Old Testament times, when there was a settling
of a contract, a shoe was removed signifying to everyone
present that an agreement had been made. Do you remember when Moses walked up to the burning bush? The first
thing God said was, "...take your shoes off" (see Exodus
3:5). God was saying to Moses, "Let's seal this thing once
and for all—take your shoes off." A sign in those times
was to take your shoe off and hold it out, which sealed
covenant from then on—stronger than any lawyer could
make it.

> **And Boaz said unto the elders, and unto all
> the people, Ye are witnesses this day, that I have
> bought all that was Elimelech's, and all that
> was Chilion's and Mahlon's, of the hand of
> Naomi.**

> **Moreover Ruth, the Moabitess, the wife of
> Mahlon, have I purchased to be my wife, to raise
> up the name of the dead upon his inheritance,
> that the name of the dead be not cut off from
> among his brethren, and from the gate of his
> place: ye are witnesses this day (Ruth 4: 9-10).**

A crowd had gathered there as Boaz, "such a one,"
and the elders were conducting their business. Boaz took
the opportunity of their presence to proclaim them as
witnesses that he had assumed responsibility for all of
Elimelech's inheritance and that he had taken Ruth to be
his wife in order to raise up children according to the
Law.

> **And all the people that were in the gate, and the elders, said, We are witnesses. The LORD make the woman that is come into thine house like Rachel and like Leah, which two did build the house of Israel: and do thou worthily in Ephrath, and be famous in Bethlehem:**
>
> **And let thy house be like the house of Pharez, whom Tamar bare unto Judah, of the seed which the LORD shall give thee of this young woman (Ruth 4: 11-12).**

You can almost hear them talking excitedly all at one time. The elders and all the people agreed with Boaz that they were witnesses to this event and they were excited about it. This was a celebration and all the people were speaking blessings over them.

Boaz Takes Ruth as His Wife

> **So Boaz took Ruth, and she was his wife: and when he went in unto her, the LORD gave her conception, and she bare a son (Ruth 4:13).**

I want you to notice something in these words. It says, **"...the LORD gave her conception..."** I am sure when she was living in Moab she had relations with her husband. The consummation of a marriage comes through a sexual encounter when the two become one flesh. So, it is obvious that she did not get pregnant in Moab. God will not add sin to sin—so he brought her out to bring her in—and now she is married to Boaz. He goes into her and the Lord gives her a baby.

Whose Baby Is It?

> And the women said unto Naomi, Blessed be the LORD, which hath not left thee this day without a kinsman, that his name may be famous in Israel.
>
> And he shall be unto thee a restorer of thy life, and a nourisher of thine old age: for thy daughter-in-law, which loveth thee, who is better to thee than seven sons, hath borne him.
>
> And Naomi took the child, and laid it in her bosom, and became nurse unto him.
>
> And the women her neighbors gave it a name, saying, There is a son born to Naomi: and they called his name Obed: he is the father of Jesse, the father of David (Ruth 4:14-17).

Who was a son born to? Who actually pushed the child out? Ruth did. Why does this say, **"...There is a son born to Naomi..." (Ruth 4:17)?** We are finding out that we may have been the vehicle, but it is really the Holy Spirit's accomplishment. Anything birthed out of us is not because of our labor—it is Him, it is the Holy Spirit, symbolized here by Naomi. This is so strange, isn't it? Ruth, the Church, gives birth but the neighbors, the cloud of witnesses, recognize the son was born to Naomi. In keeping with what we have been saying here, the reality is that the glory was given to God.

Let me tell a couple of things about the Church and where we are at right now. Conception is more fun than delivery. Think about that—conception *is* more fun than delivery. In the mid-nineties we were having conception. Do you remember the "More Lord!" we were saying over and over? It represented conception. But, we went home one night and woke up the next morning with "morning sickness." And then, the things we used to settle for were suddenly distasteful. Everything seemed to have changed overnight. It was morning sickness. A few months went by and we began to "show."

That is where the Church has been. That is why there has been so much dissatisfaction—there have been changes going on. Things are moving and spreading out. Do you understand? There has been discomfort. You can see that the Church has been "waddling" lately, but there is going to be a delivery and a birth. Just as there was a delivery with Ruth and the people understood that it wasn't Ruth, but that it was Naomi, we will understand that it isn't us, but it is the Holy Spirit.

They took the baby and laid it on the bosom of Naomi and even when they named the child they said that Naomi has had a son. If we would start giving God the credit for what He does, He would start giving us more fruit. He cannot give us fruit because we claim it all. We have all wanted something that looks just like us. We had better start birthing something that looks just like Him. The only way we can do that is by beholding Him, for when we behold Him, we become like Him (see I John 3:2). But, right now, we are reproducing after our own selves and God doesn't bless that. That's why the Church has been so barren.

Obed

**...and they called his name Obed: he is the
father of Jesse, the father of David (Ruth 4:17).**

Obed means "one with the servant's heart." Obed was
the good fruit produced out of the union of Boaz and
Ruth, symbolizing Jesus and the Church. That good fruit
was a servant. God wants to come and change the whole
philosophy of the Church. He wants us to start birthing
people who have a servant's heart. Jesus said He did not
come to be served, but He came to minister. He came to
give His life as a ransom. Many times we have said, "Oh!
Come on and get saved and become a Kingdom superstar."
No—the real way is to become a servant.

I challenge you to study the words servant and submission. Both words speak of intimacy in a relationship.
The word "servant" is from the Hebrew "Ebed" and was
used to prophetically speak of Jesus. "...for, behold, I will
bring forth my servant, the BRANCH" (see Zechariah 3:8).
The word servant not only means slave and subject, it also
means worshipper. Servants were not only slaves; they
were ambassadors, ministers, messengers, and officials.
Submission means to come up underneath and to support
that which someone else is doing. It is a picture of one
man actually holding another up to achieve some goal.
In order to support what someone else is doing, you must
be in a close relationship and know what is going on; you
are not out of the loop, just as Ananias was not out of the
loop.

In this study, it has amazed me to see how God took
Ruth out of Moab, and brought her to a city, from there

to a field, then to a corner of a field, from the corner of the field to the center of the field, from the center of the field to a threshing floor, and from a threshing floor to a city gate. And finally, He took her from a city gate to a marriage bed, and from a marriage bed to the lineage of Jesus Christ. That is amazing to me! Did you notice that the women in Ruth 4:14 prophesied? They said, **"...that his name may be famous."** Obed's name is famous, isn't it?

> **Now these are the generations of Pharez: Pharez begat Hezron,**
>
> **And Hezron begat Ram, and Ram begat Amminadab,**
>
> **And Amminadab begat Nahshon, and Nahshon begat Salmon,**
>
> **And Salmon begat Boaz, and Boaz begat Obed,**
>
> **And Obed begat Jesse, and Jesse begat David (Ruth 4:18-22).**

Yes, his name is famous. In Matthew, the first book of the New Testament, we find the entire lineage of Jesus Christ recorded. And in it we find that, **"...Salmon begat Boaz of Rachab; and Boaz begat Obed of Ruth...Mary, of whom was born Jesus, who is called Christ"** (Matthew 1:5 & 16).

I hope you will study the Book of Ruth. There are veins of truth throughout the book, and I am one hundred percent sure that it is a prophetic message to the Church.